IN THE NATIONAL INTEREST

General Sir John Monash once exhorted a graduating class to 'equip yourself for life, not solely for your own benefit but for the benefit of the whole community'. At the university established in his name, we repeat this statement to our own graduating classes, to acknowledge how important it is that common or public good flows from education.

Universities spread and build on the knowledge they acquire through scholarship in many ways, well beyond the transmission of this learning through their education. It is a necessary part of a university's role to debate its findings, not only with other researchers and scholars, but also with the broader community in which it resides.

Publishing for the benefit of society is an important part of a university's commitment to free intellectual inquiry. A university provides civil space for such inquiry by its scholars, as well as for investigations by public intellectuals and expert practitioners.

This series, In the National Interest, embodies Monash University's mission to extend knowledge and encourage informed debate about matters of great significance to Australia's future.

Professor Margaret Gardner AC
President and Vice-Chancellor,
Monash University

DON RUSSELL

LEADERSHIP

MONASH
UNIVERSITY
PUBLISHING

Leadership

Monash University Publishing
Matheson Library Annexe
40 Exhibition Walk
Monash University
Clayton, Victoria 3800, Australia
https://publishing.monash.edu

Monash University Publishing brings to the world publications which advance the best traditions of humane and enlightened thought.

ISBN: 9781922464187 (paperback)
ISBN: 9781922464200 (ebook)

Series: In the National Interest
Editor: Louise Adler
Project manager & copyeditor: Paul Smitz
Designer: Peter Long
Typesetter: Cannon Typesetting
Proofreader: Gillian Armitage
Printed in Australia by Ligare Book Printers

A catalogue record for this book is available from the National Library of Australia.

FSC
www.fsc.org
MIX
Paper from responsible sources
FSC® C011613

The paper this book is printed on is in accordance with the standards of the Forest Stewardship Council®. The FSC® promotes environmentally responsible, socially beneficial and economically viable management of the world's forests.

LEADERSHIP

It is hard to disentangle our attitude to political leadership from our general attitude to politicians. We are instinctively suspicious of their motives, but we are conscious of the fact that only from the ranks of politicians can come people capable of providing direction for how government works and impacts our lives. Sometimes our politicians are capable of great acts of leadership, while at other times they seem to have lost their way. People are often puzzled as to whether this is all in the lap of the gods or whether more is involved. The reality is that the capacity of political leaders to lead is caught up in how government itself operates. The interaction between ministers and the public service is important, as is the structure we put around ministers to help them do their jobs. In what follows, I try and shed some light on the forces at work.

My insights come from my time as principal adviser to Paul Keating while he was treasurer in the late 1980s when Bob Hawke was prime minister, and when he was prime minister himself in the early

1990s, as well as my more recent experience as a public servant heading up large government departments at both the Commonwealth and state levels. It is difficult to understand political leaders without giving some attention to the lives they lead.

LIFE AS A POLITICIAN

All political careers end badly.

This is an utterance often made, but I can attest to how it is more of an iron law than a piece of whimsy. Either the electorate will reject you or your colleagues will betray you, or if you try to anoint a hand-picked successor you will find your successor repudiates you. Even if you manage to leave on your terms, you are still likely to be seduced by delusion and go back into the burning house for the final incineration that you thought you had cleverly side-stepped. There are few exceptions. Those who escape tend to be those who can still recognise a wake-up call saying that the personal costs are getting too large.

The life of a politician is quite unnatural, being an uncomfortable combination of celebrity, conflict, power and risk. I used to watch ministers walking to the chamber for Question Time with the bells ringing, clutching their folders and with a look on their faces which said: 'Is today the day I destroy my career?'

On the outside they might look like everyone else, but politicians are different. Partly they self-select, but mainly they are the product of their experiences. As a class, they tend to be risk-lovers, which explains why so many do inexplicable things. They wear scars from a highly adversarial working environment where they are continuously subjected to savage criticism, and a career structure where the pathway to success depends on the regard of their colleagues. It is a warrior's profession, where all are surrounded by enemies—some external, and some within their own party or faction, where bitter rivals masquerade as colleagues. Some are better at hiding it, some try not to engage, and some are naturals, but as with all fighters exposed to continuous battle, the risks can take a heavy toll.

Conflict is the nature of politics. It is how countries chart a new course, set priorities, make choices and resolve disputes. To deliver, a leader needs to be able to win an argument, stare down political opponents and marginalise any opposition. A leader who delivers will earn acclaim and is well placed to build a long career. And at the end of their career, they can answer the question 'What was all that about?' by acknowledging their legacy. This is what can help rekindle long-neglected relationships. Children, partners and friends know all too well that while the career is running, there is little time for them. When the career is over, if there is no legacy, it is hard to escape the conclusion that it was all an indulgence.

There is great community cynicism about politicians. Some of this is understandable, as no-one wants to naively believe that politicians always have our best interests at heart. Many people would be hard-pressed to explain what it is that elected officials contribute. Declining support for democracy elsewhere in the world and disenchantment with political leaders in general is no doubt linked to stagnant real incomes, rising inequality and the deep divisions that are appearing in many countries. To date, Australia has avoided the worst of the overseas experience, but there is a frustration and disengagement with political leadership in our country that is disturbing. Political leaders should by nature be capable of showing the way and delivering great benefits. So why is it that there have been some periods when great acts of leadership have been possible, and others when the country has seemed unable to deal with its problems? There is a complicated story here involving how governments and decision-making are organised, but at its heart it is about what motivates our politicians.

What constitutes a legacy? Politics is a relative profession, with participants schooled in the notion that they only need to be better than their opponents to be successful. But a legacy is an absolute that needs to stand on its own—it requires broad recognition and must deliver lasting public benefit. Simply winning elections or holding high office is not enough.

It can take time to see the full significance of somebody's contribution, but a legacy without consequence is usually immediately recognisable. The absence of supportive third-party endorsements is a good indicator, and there are certain other giveaways when a politician has added little to the public good. They tend to argue that black is white, they will repeat the same three points regardless of the question, and they will have a leadership style based around obfuscation and deflection.

It is surprising that building a reputation and a legacy appears to be such a low priority for many politicians. They can be willing to lead an exceptionally harsh life, and take great risks with their personal relationships and their own wellbeing, for very little. This is puzzling behaviour.

In 2008 I was in Canberra to present the Chris Higgins Prize to the student who had achieved the best result in the Australian National University course 'Case Studies in Applied Econometrics'. As part of my prepared remarks, I made the observation that, based on my experience, which at that time was grounded in the Hawke–Keating years in Canberra, and my time in Washington as Australia's ambassador during the early Clinton years, political figures can be divided into two groups. There are those who subscribe to the notion that if you are nice to the electorate, the electorate will be nice to you. The other group tends to believe that the electorate is much more impatient, and that unless you are being useful, they will inevitably tire of you and replace you. Loosely speaking, these two groups can be described as the pleasers and the doers.

Pleasers try not to upset people and will seek approval from as many groups as possible. They will try and shield the electorate and themselves from bad news. Pleasers will be extremely interested in polling the views of people to be in a better position to please them. Doers, on the other hand, will identify problems. They tend to maintain a dialogue with the electorate and endeavour to educate and inform people. They will seek acknowledgement for tasks accomplished.

For a doer, transparency can be an asset. The identification of a problem can be the basis for their next challenge. For a pleaser, transparency can be scary. Once a problem is identified, it might need to be dealt with, which could have unpredictable and possibly painful consequences.

I have observed that doers tend to have more fun. They also get to experience the exhilarating thrill of accomplishment and the knowledge that they have done something worthwhile. Pleasers find it hard to gain acknowledgement and live the life of a thousand miseries.

A RETURN TO PUBLIC POLICY

In early 2011 I received a phone call from Terry Moran, then secretary of the Department of the Prime Minister and Cabinet (PM&C). Terry asked me to come to Canberra to talk to him about becoming the new secretary of the Industry Department; I would also need to talk to the minister, Kim Carr. Terry hoped that I would not dismiss the suggestion out of hand. In fact, after fifteen years spent working in asset management and superannuation, this call would take me back to public policy and public sector administration in two jurisdictions, although at the time I did not realise that there would be a second leg to my journey.

When Kim Carr asked me why I wanted to return to Canberra to work for him, I remember saying that I could see how, as the industry minister, he wanted to leave a legacy, and that I was happy to help him build it. I added that a legacy cannot be built on nonsense. I also acknowledged the ironies of my return, given my involvement in the reforms of the 1980s and early 1990s which, among other things, had led to a drastic reduction in industry protection.

And so, in mid-2011, some twenty-six years after I had left the Commonwealth Treasury to become treasurer Paul Keating's principal private secretary, I was appointed secretary of the then Department of Innovation, Industry, Science and Research by Julia Gillard, Australia's first female prime minister. Later, in 2014, I would find myself in Adelaide after being appointed the chief executive of the then Department of State Development (DSD) by Jay Weatherill, who had won a surprising fourth term for his Labor government. Both these departments were large, recently merged entities with many ministers. Both were focused on economic transformation. At the federal level, the driver was the resources boom. An explosion in mining investment was driving up incomes and wealth across the country. But it was also driving up the exchange rate, which in 2011 reached 1.10 against the US dollar. This spike was decimating manufacturing—while shaking out marginal companies, it was also forcing the closure of companies normally considered highly competitive. The challenge at the South Australian level was compounded by the closure of Holden, which was scheduled for October 2017.

When I arrived, the federal department was already committed to the notion that industry policy was innovation policy; the South Australian department still had a way to go on this. Regardless, putting together skills, research, science, universities, innovation and industry accelerated the natural synergies that existed between these responsibilities in both jurisdictions. The two big departments owed their structure to the wishes of the prime minister and the state premier. They helped to reduce turf battles and create a single point of accountability around a key government policy objective.

The two departments had similar structures in that they involved many ministers but only one public service head. In total, I had good working relationships with twelve ministers in Canberra and nine in Adelaide, including the premier and deputy premier.[1] In Adelaide, I also had Cabinet responsibilities when I became chief executive of the Department of the Premier and Cabinet in February 2017.

During my time in Canberra, there was considerable ministerial movement as bitterness around who should lead the government took its toll. However, dealing with the economic consequences of a high exchange rate and the need to put in place a mechanism to deal with climate change remained areas of strong focus. When I joined the federal Industry Department, it already had responsibility for the research side of universities, and in December 2011, responsibility for the rest of the universities and for training were added. In March 2013, the old Climate Change Department was disbanded and most of its functions were added to my department.

Change was the order of the day. The brief for incoming ministers needed to be constantly updated. Early on, my ministers were on both sides of the leadership divide, but as time went on there were large-scale departures and arrivals as one side or the other found itself in the ascendancy. The rapid turnover put extra pressure on the department to help maintain the continuity of the federal government's program. But the ministers appeared capable of compartmentalising their lives, plotting in private while maintaining professional proprieties. They accepted the logic of the big department and, notwithstanding leadership tensions, they were willing for me to manage the department in a way that made best use of the potential synergies. Making the whole bigger than the sum of the parts was an accepted ambition.

In Adelaide, Cabinet collegiality was stronger, but with the imminent closure of Holden hanging over the city, the economic imperatives were greater. The urgency of the economic task for the state was reflected in the broad responsibilities of the new DSD. As well as linking training, innovation, science and industry, DSD also took on responsibility for Indigenous affairs, the arts, minerals and energy, and investment and trade. It was a clear signal that the state government intended to make economic progress its paramount objective.

After his 2014 election victory, Weatherill was able to renew his Cabinet, adding a number of younger ministers. Notwithstanding the presence of two independents, the Cabinet members worked well together and appeared to have a measure of affection for each other.[2] After my experience in Canberra, this was refreshing.

HOW HAVE THINGS CHANGED?

Today, it is still possible to broadly divide political figures into pleasers and doers. However, the framework in which ministers operate has changed and the situation is now more complex. I have come across ministers who clearly have the instinct of a doer but find themselves constrained by the disciplines placed on them by those responsible for political strategy. These people are usually close to the prime minister and can include key ministers, but often they are staff in the Prime Minister's Office (PMO) or from the party.

In 2008, I acknowledged that the division between pleasers and doers was not binary and that there were gradations. I would now emphasise the gradations and say that political leaders lie on a continuum, and if it is accepted that Paul Keating is the consummate doer, then all politicians have some Keating within them.

Related to the new disciplines for ministers is the rise in the importance of polling. There are now many who instinctively believe that politicians should take their cues from the observed views of the electorate. At its extreme, this belief has people testing policy options, narratives, even words through polling before political parties embrace a particular approach. These people are pleasers—polling has enabled their preferred approach to be weaponised and imposed on others.

To understand what political leadership means in the current context, we must consider changes to the framework in which ministers operate. There are three key influences here: the role of ministerial staff, the public service, and communicating with the public.

THE MINISTERIAL ADVISER

The prime minister of the day and the PMO spend a large amount of their time managing individual ministers and dealing with their problems.[3] This has been a longstanding issue with the Australian Cabinet. Using a cricket analogy, Ben Chifley spoke of the long tail of the batting line-up of his ministerial colleagues. Robert Menzies, too, had doubts about the calibre of his

Cabinet. Having a diversity of talent in the Cabinet is not necessarily a bad thing, but it needs to be managed.

Chifley liked to be surrounded by clever people who could achieve things, and the post–World War II elite of department secretaries in Canberra was the result. To Menzies, who inherited Chifley's public service, it was preferable to have the power in Canberra in the hands of a cadre of talented high officials answerable to him, rather than to have it dissipated through a collection of ministers for whom he had only modest regard.

The next generation of secretaries misunderstood the basis of their power. They overreached and produced a bipartisan consensus that the policy agenda belonged with ministers, that ministers should be equipped to develop policy proposals, and that they should no longer be hostage to powerful officials who dictated what was and what was not acceptable. Dating from Gough Whitlam, then reinforced by Malcolm Fraser and every subsequent prime minister, the result has been a growing pool of powerful and influential advisers in ministerial offices.

The *Members of Parliament (Staff) Act 1984*—or *MOP(S)*—was particularly important as it allowed for the employment of ministerial staff separate from the Australian Public Service (APS)—public servants could be employed under *MOP(S)* and then return to the APS. During the Hawke–Keating years, there was a large increase in the number of ministerial staff, with the total rising from around 210 to about 350.[4] The pool of ministerial staff has since only gotten bigger; under Scott Morrison, it stands at around 450.[5]

Prime ministers and premiers still need to coordinate and manage the government's agenda. To do this, they need to be in a position where they can encourage ministers to do some things and stop them from doing others. The PMO at the Commonwealth level and the premier's office at the state level have stepped up to perform this role and, in the process, they have transformed how governments work in all jurisdictions. Prime ministers expect to have advisers who cover all areas of government, and a well-managed PMO will work collegially and with a sense of purpose, although that is not always the case. The net result is that, for every minister, there is someone in the PMO keeping an eye on them. If anything, the overriding authority of the PMO has increased over the years.

The dynamics of ministers' offices, meanwhile, can be quite daunting and are difficult to manage. It has been said that some offices verge on dysfunctional, and that attracting talented staff can be hard. Overwhelmed ministers with confused and inadequate staff can wreak great damage on any government, hence trying to strengthen their offices, particularly those of struggling ministers, has increasingly become a preoccupation of chiefs of staff at both the federal and state/territory levels.

The basic nature of ministerial offices has not altered that much since the Hawke–Keating years, with the forces at work much the same as they have always been. What has changed is the nature and backgrounds of the staff. In the years after my return to public policy in 2011, I worked with twenty-odd ministerial offices, as well as a premier's office and the PMO. What struck me was the diminished number of public servants across these offices. In the 1980s and 1990s, public servants on secondment would play a much more significant role.[6] In fact, it was common practice for the head of a minister's office to be a relatively senior public servant.

Graham Evans, a branch head from the Treasury with a foreign affairs background, was Bob Hawke's first principal adviser, or chief of staff. He told me that Hawke expected his ministers to have good relations with the public service and to have experienced public service advisers in their offices. The fact that, in 1980, Hawke had pre-emptively indicated to Evans his preference for a senior public servant to head up the PMO, and had asked Evans regarding his interest if Hawke were to become PM, when Evans was attached to the Washington embassy and Hawke was in the US capital as an Opposition backbencher, was evidence of a man with a heavy sense of destiny—not to mention someone who'd thought about what it would mean to run an effective and successful government.[7] Early on, Evans was instrumental in recruiting Ross Garnaut and John Bowen to the PMO as Hawke's economic and foreign policy advisers, respectively.

When Keating became treasurer, he was keen to have a Treasury official of standing head up his own office. He wanted someone who understood Treasury—who knew where the bodies were buried, as he would say—and was loyal to him. And so Tony Cole, an assistant secretary in that department, became Keating's first principal adviser. Two years later, Cole's last responsibility was to suggest a successor. He recommended me, and after an interview with Keating I took over.

Keating was keen to have a wide range of people in his office who could provide him with ideas and oversight an ambitious reform agenda. He wanted talent that could feed his never-ending curiosity and help him pull ideas into a compelling narrative.[8] He did not mind where the talent came from; they just needed to know their material and think clearly and imaginatively. Keating found much of this talent within the public service in Canberra, but he was happy to look further afield. Keating had—and still has—the mind of a gifted Queen's Counsel. He took raw ideas and assembled them into a powerful story that he used to build support for change and wrong-foot his political opponents.

Unlike his predecessors, Keating was not concerned that Treasury would overwhelm him with information. Rather, he was at ease dropping into the department to talk to officials about any topic in which he had an interest. Right from the start, he was also a strong advocate of ministers locating themselves in their departments rather than being locked up with the press gallery in the hothouse of Parliament House. The notion that the main role of a minister's office was to take an adversarial stance with their department seemed misguided to Keating—the department was a resource and the role of the minister's office was to extract this value.

Hawke and Keating used policy formulation and delivery as a key part of their political strategies, both in terms of delivering for the electorate and marginalising the Opposition. This approach meant that policy was the currency of exchange around Parliament House. If ministers wanted to be noticed, they, too, needed a policy agenda and the capacity to articulate and deliver it. There was strong pressure on all ministers to appoint experienced policy people, and many drew advisers from the public service to fill this role.

The Hawke–Keating era also saw a dramatic change in the way government operated in Australia. There were significant changes to employment conditions for ministerial staff—salaries were lifted to levels more in keeping with those of senior executives in the APS—while at the same time it was made clear that ministers were expected to be actively pursuing a policy agenda. The new arrangements worked extremely well for Hawke and Keating. Not only were ministers equipped with a highly effective way of driving policy change, key departments were able to work productively with ministers to put in place reforms that had languished for decades. It was very much a virtuous circle. Reputations were enhanced, the country was strengthened, and between them, Hawke and Keating won five elections in a row.

As academic researchers have noted, the Australian system of ministerial advisers is unusual in that not only are they large in number, they have been accepted as part of the political landscape.[9] Other developed democracies operate with political advisers, but few have as many as Australia, and in most other countries their existence remains a source of debate. In the United Kingdom, the role of special advisers, or temporary civil servants—UK civil servants do not work as special advisers on secondment—is contentious and subject to resistance. The Canadians have many political advisers but less of a tradition of public servants moving in and out of ministerial offices as policy advisers.[10] The Americans, meanwhile, ban the use of separate political advisers for members of Cabinet, preferring to opt for a model where the Senior Executive Service changes from one administration to another, and each president selects their White House staff. No-one else has gone quite as far as Australia with an institutionalised structure where career public servants and other policy advisers can become part of a minister's private office while remaining quite separate to the public service, and with this structure generally accepted as part of the machinery of government.

The original motivation for the Australian model was to give ministers the capacity to develop policy options separate from the advice coming from the public service. Both Hawke and Keating gave such a high priority to tidy processes and imaginative policy development, so ministers originally appointed people from the public service. This worked well for the ministers, for the political fortunes of the government, and for policy outcomes. The important question now is, what does it mean to surround ministers with influential advisers who, by and large, no longer have public service or policy experience?

I have a developing fear that, when it comes to ministerial staff, we have provided ministers with a cornucopia of opportunities which, because of prevailing attitudes, is more likely to hamstring political leadership and deliver distressingly inadequate results, as opposed to the exceptional outcomes that we associate with Hawke and Keating.

To elaborate, many advisers now see their role quite differently from that performed by advisers in the Hawke–Keating years. Time in a minister's office has always been viewed as a potential pathway to preselection and a political career, and Parliament House is clearly a strategic place to network and to look for powerful mentors. However, the possibility of preselection for a House or Senate seat has not been a major motivator for career public servants recruited by ministers. The dramatic reduction in the number of public servants in ministers' offices has meant that there are now many more advisers thinking of the time when they too will sit on the other side of the desk.

There are also now more advisers who see themselves as career ministerial staffers. Some move between state and Commonwealth roles; some consider themselves factionally aligned and expect to be looked after as ministers come and go; some see themselves as subject specialists; and some see themselves as generalists with an interest in political tactics, communications or speechwriting. Some find themselves in a minister's office as a result of a factional deal over preselection. There are even some who see themselves as political strategists. Many are highly experienced and well networked and can be of useful service to their minister. The best are trusted and have the capacity to anticipate problems, apply sound judgement, and protect their minister from the constant wear and tear of political life.

What these advisers are not are people experienced in public sector probity, administration and policymaking. Few can harness the strengths of the public service to the benefit of the minister. Those who do have accumulated experience with the public service often carry scars from times when they have felt misled or betrayed. Many believe that the APS is part of the problem and instinctively take up an adversarial approach when dealing with their public service contacts.

It is hard to generalise about ministerial offices, but all revolve around the minister and take on much of that person's personality. Also common is the pressure of the immediate. The problems of the day will push out almost anything else, until that too becomes a problem. An awkward inquiry from a journalist might be a problem, as might an irate call from a stakeholder. A departmental mistake could be a problem compounded if the inquiry from the journalist and the stakeholder were linked to it. Worst of all, the inquiry from the journalist might first go to the prime minister or premier's press secretary. The problem may involve another minister or another department that is refusing to cooperate. Or it could originate with the prime minister or premier, who has tasked the minister with finding a solution and now has their staff following this up. There will be ongoing budget fights over much of the minister's programs, and any notion of new money will depend on a complex interplay of the offices of the prime minister or premier and the treasurer. Overlaying all of this will be the immediate needs of the minister regarding briefings, or their Cabinet papers and Question Time folder, along with a copy of the speech they are giving at breakfast the next morning. And, of course, all of these problems will be occurring at the same time.

Little of this is likely to add to the minister's legacy. Which begs the question: how would things be different if the office included experienced, executive-level public servants, or people with a public policy background? It is likely that the presence of such people would reduce the number of problems that the office or minister cause or stumble into. More importantly, people with public policy experience and the capacity to drive an agenda give the minister the scope to pursue options that are not prompted by the immediate problems of the day. Whether a minister would choose such options is another matter, which I will explore later.

Those ministers who decide to head up their offices with an experienced public servant have tended to be more successful than those who do not. The stand-out success in this regard was Greg Combet, who chose Allan Behm, an experienced senior Defence official, as his chief of staff. Greg Combet was tasked by his prime minister, Julia Gillard, to develop and implement the *Clean Energy Act 2011*, a major piece of Commonwealth legislation that I discuss later in this book. Those familiar with the Hawke–Keating era would have found the Combet office very recognisable.

An office overly staffed with people experienced in conflict, crisis management and short-term political responsiveness will tend to approach everything from that perspective. Understandably, people view problems from the prism of their own experiences and will often seek to replicate past successes. Without the capacity to see the broader context, even a well-managed office, one adept at dealing with problems, will leave the minister adrift, with a limited ability to proactively control their destiny. Building a network of advice around ministers that restricts their capacity to think beyond the immediate does them no favours. It also weakens governments and certainly undermines the political process in delivering for the community.

THE PUBLIC SERVICE AND THE ROLE OF THE SECRETARY

The APS had an important role to play during the Hawke–Keating years, but it was a role that was very much coordinated, and validated, by a group of trusted senior public servants who occupied key positions in the offices of the prime minister, treasurer and other key ministers. In more recent years, as the role and background of ministerial advisers have changed, there has been a general level of antagonism towards the public service, a willingness to believe that the APS is a problem that needs to be confronted and addressed.

In talking about the current role of the public service and that of the department secretary or head of department, a good starting point is the reform agenda recently announced by Prime Minister Morrison.

In December 2019, Morrison released *Delivering for Australians*, which laid out the government's APS reform agenda.[11] The publication also embodied the government's response to the Thodey Review of the public service, which was released at the same time and made forty recommendations.[12] In stating that 'It is Ministers who provide policy leadership and direction', Morrison was simply declaring what all Australian prime ministers since Whitlam have taken as an article of faith: ministers will not be dictated to by public servants. The overreach of the secretaries from fifty-odd years ago continues to reverberate to this day.[13]

Recommendation 11 of the Thodey Review called for the federal government to set guidance for ministerial offices for at least half of their policy advisers to have public service experience. This was rejected by the government, as were recommendations seeking to amend the *Public Service Act*, enshrining new principles of openness and integrity (recommendation 5); give new powers to the APS commissioner (recommendation 7); make systematic changes to Cabinet and budget processes (recommendation 26); establish an Integrated Strategy Office in PM&C (recommendation 28); evaluate the machinery of government changes (recommendation 30); set common pay scales across the APS (recommendation 33); review and amend the Charter of Budget Honesty (recommendation 36); strengthen the legislation underpinning the Secretaries Board (recommendation 37); amend the *Public Service Act* to reinforce the leadership roles of the head of PM&C, the APS commissioner and portfolio secretaries (recommendation 38); build more process around the appointment of agency heads (recommendation 39a); and establish more robust processes around the termination of secretaries (recommendation 39c).

Essentially, the government rejected recommendations which appeared to give the public service new powers to constrain the behaviour of ministers and the prime minister. Given the adversarial stance of both major parties towards the public service when in office, the government's response was not that surprising. Prime ministers do not like to be hemmed in when it comes to appointing or dismissing secretaries, nor are they keen on increasing their powers in an ill-defined way. Add constraints on who can be appointed under *MOP(S)*, and extra scrutiny of the prime minister's ability to reshuffle departmental responsibilities, and many of the recommendations become less than appealing to those who will have to make the decision to implement.

In responding to the Thodey Review, Prime Minister Morrison reframed the task somewhat, emphasising the clear division between ministers and the APS, and the key role that the APS has in getting service delivery to Australians right. There was much emphasis on APS performance targets and the better use of data to improve outcomes and accountability. It was interesting that the Prime Minister's response put great store in the Secretaries Board, providing it and the APS Commission (APSC) with significant new funding to commence reforms.[14] Having dismissed the need for legislation to drive behaviour, the Prime

Minister was supportive of reform as long as it was pursued within the confines of existing channels.

In his response to Thodey, the Prime Minister also recognised the Commonwealth's involvement in expanding new areas such as the National Disability Insurance Scheme, aged care, mental health and suicide prevention. As opposed to traditional Commonwealth service-delivery responsibilities such as pension payments, which rest on large, systems-based platforms, these new areas involve highly discretionary engagement with people and are more akin to the service-delivery responsibilities of the states. As is all too familiar to state ministers and premiers, things can go wrong when public servants need to use their judgement or are oversighting private providers and vulnerable people are involved. And when things go wrong, they can go wrong in an unconscionable way that brings a firestorm of public scrutiny. Ministers, ministerial offices and public servants get caught in an ugly melee involving royal commissions, corruption commissions and maladministration cases, processes that can be very damaging to them—to say nothing of the vulnerable members of the public who find that the system has failed them at a moment of great need.[15]

I suspect that Commonwealth ministers today are in the process of entering a world of pain, already familiar to state ministers, for which they are not well prepared. COVID-19 and its impact on aged care has already made the Commonwealth minister a focus of attention. I would anticipate that this level of scrutiny will be more damaging the more adversarial the nature of the relationship between ministers and public servants.

Which brings me back to the core questions: What is the role of the public service and what is the role of the departmental secretary? And how is this related to political leadership and successful outcomes for governments and the community?

In 2014, I observed that only the secretaries can save the APS. In building up to this conclusion, I also noted that secretaries have more authority than they think.[16] Since then, I have had the benefit of working as a chief executive at the state level with a new group of ministers and a premier, as well as engaging with my counterparts across jurisdictions, including the Commonwealth. In South Australia, I also had overarching responsibility for the public service in my role as head of the premier's department, which saw me chairing the Senior Management Council and the State Emergency Management Committee, and taking an active role in the performance assessment of my chief executive colleagues.[17]

My core belief in the importance of the secretary has not changed, nor have my views on how secretaries should approach their job. Where my thinking has evolved is around the skills required of a successful secretary or head of a government department. I have also given thought as to whether there is something special about the abilities required of the head of the prime minister's or premier's department.

The task facing a modern secretary is simply huge. The trend of ever-larger merged departments has continued in recent times, with Prime Minister Morrison reducing the number of Commonwealth departments from eighteen to fourteen in December 2019. In the process, he terminated the appointments of five existing secretaries and reappointed Andrew Metcalfe, who had himself been fired in 2013.[18] There are important scale economies with large departments which partly explains mergers. The more significant reason is that all bureaucracies tend to form silos, and those silos become citadels when they are located in different departments protected by separate ministers. Turf battles become more intractable, people learn that intransigence can be rewarded, and unless care is taken, the situation can deteriorate to the point where people in different departments can see themselves as belonging to different tribes.

The benefit of internalising differences within one department is that a single secretary can provide a mechanism with which to resolve disputes.

Paralysing disagreements become less common when those so inclined have to answer to a secretary who signs their employment contracts and conducts their performance reviews. The attraction to a prime minister or premier of merging departments is that it gives them a powerful apparatus to link those parts of the government that need to cooperate to achieve goals. If the prime minister or premier has high confidence in the secretary who is chosen to lead the merged department, then this is an additional attraction. As Jay Weatherill said to me in Adelaide, the alternative to coordinating matters in one department is to have them coordinated by ministers around the Cabinet table—a task not necessarily playing to ministers' strongest skill set.

However, it is not inevitable that merging departments leads to big efficiency gains. Much rests on the skill and determination of the secretary. In Canberra, we had a measure of success with the Department of Industry, Innovation, Climate Change, Science, Research and Tertiary Education, but it took relentless engagement with the staff, explaining the rationale for the big department.

Securing a benefit from having many responsibilities located in a single large department is only one of the challenges facing the modern secretary. There are, in fact, two additional capabilities that have to be mastered. The first, and most important, is the ability to work effectively with ministers.[19] This is a complicated task, for which a career working in a government department is not necessarily the best preparation. The second is the capability to work effectively with the head of PM&C, because the prime minister's power to hire and fire creates an implied dotted line from that person to all secretaries.[20] An impaired capacity to master either of these two additional challenges is likely to be career-limiting.

The question then becomes: who has the ability to manage huge, multifaceted departments while forging effective relationships with potentially multiple ministers, while also working effectively with the head of the prime minister's or premier's department? And how should we view these heads?

Time spent in a minister's office is one of the few experiences that a public servant can obtain that will prepare them for the role of secretary. With one exception, all public servants report to somebody else. For everyone other than the secretary, there is a direct report who can clear anything that might appear contentious. This might be clumsy, but it is comforting. However, taking on the role of secretary means that, for the first time in their career, public servants can find themselves entirely responsible for any position they take—that is, if they have not worked in a minister's office, for advisers are expected to take positions every day that will come back to haunt them if they are wrong. Furthermore, a stint in a ministerial office does not just prepare people for taking responsibility. It also provides direct experience with ministers, with how they think and behave and work together. Importantly, it provides experience in how to maintain a trusted relationship while disagreeing with the ultimate decision-maker where all you have is your reputation, and in how to do this in a potentially unstructured or highly time-constrained environment. Time spent in a minister's office can also be helpful experience for a secretary appearing before a Senate estimates committee.

People sometimes express concern that public servants returning from a minister's office could bring partisan attitudes that do not sit well with an apolitical APS. The right to return needs to be honoured; however, if former advisers behave inappropriately, there are mechanisms ranging from counselling to performance management that can be used. Returning advisers will be keen to demonstrate that their time in the minister's office has strengthened them as a public servant, not weakened their capacity to behave according to the APS code of conduct. There are circumstances where advisers, who are not public servants, apply for open positions in the minister's department. Good people can enter the APS in this way, but the selection process in such cases needs to be rigorous. The secretary is responsible for staffing matters within the department, and in all situations involving returning public servants or the appointment of advisers, they need to pay close attention. No secretary would want to agree to arrangements that they view as inappropriate.

It is interesting that of the fourteen secretaries attached to the new line-up of departments announced by Prime Minister Morrison in December 2019, nine have spent time in a minister's office earlier in their career and six have been chiefs of staff. Importantly, the offices involved are from both sides of politics.[21] It is possible to view this development in two ways. Either we may be edging towards resolving a gaping weakness in the Australian system of political governance, or it is further evidence of the frustration that prime ministers and ministers have with the public service.

Let's take the more optimistic view first. To better understand the weakness in our political governance, consider Daniel Kahneman's 2012 book *Thinking, Fast and Slow*.[22] It is clear that the public service is by its very nature a Slow Thinking organisation—it values reason and considered analysis. However, the public service is answerable to ministers who, by their very nature, have a capacity, and a need, for

Fast Thinking—they are intuitive and warriors by instinct and trade. Our system is indeed a strange one. Unlike the United States, where the legislature is quite separate from the executive, in Australia ministers have executive authority vested in them. We expect them to think beyond the immediate, make careful decisions, care about the circumstances of the nation, and plan ahead. In the end we will judge them entirely on this contribution. But they are also fighters. The best of them can do both. They have developed a proficiency in Slow Thinking while maintaining an intuitive ability for Fast Thinking; where rapid response is essential, instinct needs to take over. In effect, the best can restructure the financial system in their head while dealing with the Opposition leader in Question Time.

In 2014, Gareth Evans published a book which reinforced Kahneman's insights.[23] Back in September 1984, Evans started writing a daily Cabinet diary. It was a testing time for the senator. The day before he started writing, he lost preselection for a House seat, and his time as attorney-general was proving problematic—this after having gained national notoriety for arranging for the RAAF to take surveillance photos of the Franklin Dam in Tasmania. Much to his dismay, in December 1984, after the federal election, he was transferred out of the Attorney-General portfolio to Resources and Energy. As he says in the introduction to his diary, if he was to be relegated to the sidelines, he may as well write about it like the British Labour MP Richard Crossman.

The diary covers only two years of a thirteen-year ministerial career, and Evans left it undisturbed for nearly three decades. He was finally encouraged to publish because of a continuing fascination with what made the Hawke–Keating government tick. It is a good read, but it does not answer that question. What it does highlight is that, notwithstanding the extraordinary talent residing in the Hawke–Keating Cabinet between 1984 and 1986, in terms of the passions of individual members, they were very much like any other group of ministers that I have observed. The quality of the back-and-forth may have been better, but the interests of the ministers were much the same as today: recognition, promotion, preselection and power.

Evans is conscious of the problem. In his introduction he poses the following questions about the Hawke–Keating Cabinet:

> How, exactly, did it manage to do so much amid all the endless distracting clashes of egos and agendas that, then as now, so dominate Australian political life? How did this highly strung collection of very capable, very forceful personalities ever manage to work together as a team?[24]

This is the Kahneman-prompted dilemma writ large. How do you ensure that a group of big personalities, who have become accustomed to thinking instinctively, do not get distracted but instead deliver an agenda that is built on reason and considered analysis?

I was in Parliament House heading up Keating's office for the second half of Evans's diary and I am probably better placed than he to understand why the Hawke–Keating Cabinet was so productive, even though Evans was actually in the Cabinet at the time. Evans was probably aware that there were advisers in key ministers' offices with senior public service backgrounds, but I suspect he did not fully appreciate what they did. Essentially, these were experienced public servants with the trust of the prime minister, treasurer and ministers, and motivated to facilitate the implementation of an agenda that they believed in. They were well coordinated, not only with each other but with key departments and agencies. They had the experience and the capability to drive change through the public service, but they were also able, because of their trusted status, to expand the menu of options that was put before the prime minister and the treasurer. Notwithstanding the endless disorder of Parliament House, the frenetic scrutiny of the media, and the savagery of the political onslaught on the government at that time, there was a discipline around the Cabinet that enabled it to successfully pursue an ambitious agenda of change.

The important takeaway from this period is that this discipline was not imposed on the government but came directly from the choices made by Hawke and Keating, the primary one being Hawke's original decision to have a senior public servant head up his office. What that meant was that Hawke had the benefit of wise counselling on all important proposals for change, and there were many, which delivered great dividends. Initially, I was unsure as to whether this arrangement came from luck or design, but having heard from Graham Evans about how he was appointed as the PM's principal adviser, I have come to the conclusion that Hawke thought carefully about how to run a successful government.[25] The disarray of the Whitlam years was a powerful motivator, as was the need to dispel any notions that Hawke himself lacked personal discipline. The upshot was that Hawke understood that effective government required discipline and a considered approach to developing policy.

Chifley, confronted by the challenges of post–World War II reconstruction, concluded that he wanted the process driven by a talented pool of clever secretaries handpicked by him, and which could then draw on a network of experts around the country. In doing this, he was building on the lessons learnt from the war years. The Cabinet sat at the centre of the reconstruction effort, but Chifley did not think it was a good idea to allow the instincts and passions of individual members to drive what his government did. Chifley's arrangement with the secretaries also worked well for Menzies, but the next generation of secretaries took it upon themselves to constrain not only the behaviour of ministers but that of the prime minister himself. This led to a fraying of the authority of the secretaries and the public service, and to the rise of contestable advice coming from advisers.

Hawke and Keating took this to another level, providing ministers with additional resources and new hiring arrangements that enabled them to attract a wide range of experts who could drive a sophisticated reform agenda. However, they, too, deliberately constrained the behaviour of ministers by populating their own offices with senior public servants, and they encouraged other ministers to do the same. They empowered ministers to pursue an agenda but they did not let them, or themselves for that matter, run free. The net result was hugely beneficial to the country—accelerated, imaginative change during a time of economic difficulty. Hawke, Keating and their ministers were able to transform the country in a manner determined by them, and to have the consequent success acknowledged and firmly attributed to their leadership. For political leaders, it does not get much better.

To answer the Gareth Evans question, I am confident that if the Hawke–Keating Cabinet had been surrounded by advisers similar to those who have populated ministers' offices more recently, it would have delivered outcomes more in keeping with what we expect from governments today than what they actually achieved.

Which brings me back to the challenges of today and Prime Minister Morrison's current line-up of secretaries. First, any Commonwealth minister with state government–like service-delivery responsibilities would be well advised to appoint a trusted, experienced public servant to head up their office. They would also be well advised to make sure that they not only trust and respect their secretary, but that they are confident that this person fully understands what is going on in the department—and can not only identify existing and potential problems, but also rectify them. The risks, after all, are high, and choosing not to work closely with the secretary and instead running an adversarial relationship with the department is likely to heighten that risk.

Second, all prime ministers have the authority to determine the type of government they lead and how it functions. Various prime ministers have done this in quite different circumstances to the benefit of the country and their own personal standing. The current stripped-down number of secretaries, many of whom have extensive experience in working with ministers, has the potential to build new, constructive ministerial relationships, just as there is the scope to build departments that are viewed as imaginative sources of advice and accepted as operating with good administrative practices. Such arrangements work best when talented outside experts are at hand. It is unclear as to whether today's ministers are in a position to appoint outside experts to their offices of the calibre of those appointed during the Hawke–Keating years, but this should be explored.[26]

It is true that in a world with high expectations concerning the performance of secretaries, and where success is highly subjective and linked to a secretary's ability to work effectively with ministers, prime ministers and the secretary of PM&C, it is inevitable that there are going to be casualties, often in situations where the secretary has no real understanding of why their services are no longer required.[27] Indeed, secretaries at the Commonwealth level are well compensated and there are provisions for the breaking of contracts—it is also legitimate to say that secretaries are paid danger money. However, there does need to be recognition that someone who has a demonstrated ability to run a large and complicated department, make sense of public sector processes, and build productive relationships with ministers and their offices, as well as work successfully with colleagues, has an unusual skill set, and that the universe of people with these skills is small.

The PM appoints the secretaries. They should be people that the PM knows, respects and trusts, and the head of PM&C should be the conduit for ensuring that there is a coherence around how departments operate. If any prime minister ever wants to leverage up their influence, it is there waiting to be activated through the secretary of PM&C. For this to work, the person whom the prime minister appoints to head up their department needs to be a person of standing, someone who believes in the APS and who can garner respect from other secretaries and the public service at large. Such a person needs to not only have the trust of the prime minister but also some understanding of what the PM is trying to accomplish.

The more-optimistic perspective on Scott Morrison's changes to the public service in December 2019 is that we may be developing the basis for revisiting the Chifley model of effective government—without, of course, unleashing a new generation of unaccountable secretaries. This would provide a mechanism to deal with the Kahneman-prompted dilemma that there is a basic disconnect between the frenetic world ministers inhabit and the patient world of policy analysis and formulation. It is a disconnect that needs to be resolved because it damages not only the ministers but the community to whom the ministers are ultimately answerable.

The less optimistic view is much bleaker. It would suggest that we are witnessing accumulated frustration being asserted through the appointment of a range of minister-friendly secretaries whose brief is to bring public servants to heel and channel their energies largely into efficient service provision and policy implementation.

I am an optimist. I believe that people who work in the public service overwhelmingly want to make a difference, and that it is in everyone's interests to make the public service work for ministers and all Australians. But at the end of the day, this is a matter for the prime minister. If they accept that their own and their ministers' performances will only be as good as the structure of governance they put around themselves, and the advice that flows from that, then we need to change the habits of recent years and create something that works.

Getting the governance right would be a major step forward, one that would improve the capacity of prime ministers and ministers to lead and successfully deal with problems, but it is not the end of the story.

There is also a need to view a government's attitude to policy differently and incorporate it into a party's political strategy. Hawke and Keating put policy change centrestage, treating it as an integral part of their political strategy.

WHO IS LISTENING?

Returning to Canberra in 2011, I found it odd how many resources were devoted to getting attention. Ministers were preoccupied with finding journalists to talk to or radio identities to chat with. Featuring on any of the main free-to-air TV channels was a matter of some moment. Bloomberg TV, Sky News, European news channels—all were valued. In fact, any form of media was treated seriously. Moving to Adelaide, I found that the preoccupation with media there was even greater. Ministers were active on Twitter, departments were also focused on social media, and individual public servants got satisfaction from the attention they received on LinkedIn. All the ministers seemed to have press secretaries, whereas in the Hawke–Keating years, considerable effort had gone into ensuring that only the prime minister, treasurer and a fortunate other few had them. And while I had been away, a whole industry had grown up producing glossy brochures. It seemed that no policy announcement was complete without such a brochure, with its mandatory cheery photographs of happy families, trees and sunshine.

But despite all this effort, it was hard to get the media's attention. And the reality was that if a minister was the centre of attention, it was usually for the wrong reasons.

The contrast with my earlier stint with Keating could not have been starker. At that time, journalists hung on every nuance—it was not a question of getting journalists to pay attention, it was a question of keeping them at bay. It was different then, of course, in that the federal government was in the process of turning the country upside down, which automatically drew attention. However, Keating approached the media in a different way from that of ministers today. His starting point was—and still is—that access to a national audience is a priceless opportunity that should not be wasted. He always told people something interesting that helped them better understand that what he was doing was worthy and good for the country. He was a tireless advocate, even to the extent of carrying topical economic charts on the off-chance he might meet a journalist. He could engage with the Canberra press gallery such that, for much of the time, he had the broad support of informed opinion. I have always given the journalists in the press gallery back then, like Michael Stutchbury, Steve Burrell and

Laura Tingle, credit for their role in helping people comprehend what the issues were during Australia's golden years of public policy.

It is not just that ministers today approach the media differently from Keating. There have also been enormous structural changes. The press gallery has shrunk. Digital disruption has severely damaged the business model that supports newspapers, and the capacity to hire experienced journalists is in steep decline. The proportion of the populace watching news programs is falling. For many people, the news they receive comes filtered through social media. We have been steadily transforming the old media notion of *one to many*, with its implication of control, with the notion of *many to many*, which can politely be described as the democratisation of news but can also be seen as the arming of the mob.

In such a world, it is understandable that political leaders and ministers would dearly like to know what is on peoples' minds before they talk to them, or make policy decisions, or in fact do anything. Polling performs this function. The attraction of polling is that it appears to hold out the prospect of increasing the probability that something a politician says, or a policy approach or action, might be well received. It is a seductive notion, but one fraught with danger. To start with, the level of public cynicism is so high now that people instinctively distrust what politicians say and do, assuming that it is self-serving, insincere and manipulative. If the primary driver of a politician's actions were in fact poll-driven, then such cynicism would, of course, be warranted. But the real problem with polling is that peoples' views are not that well defined.

Referring back to Daniel Kahneman, 'your actions and your emotions can be primed by events of which you are not even aware'.[28] Even more problematic, our Fast Thinking or intuitive response 'is designed to jump to conclusions from little evidence and considering how little we know, the confidence we have in our beliefs is preposterous'.[29] This means that views that appear firmly held in the polling can change materially as circumstances change and other views enter the public debate. It is now well accepted that the beliefs people have are not internally consistent, and that we are comfortable having strong views about things that are at odds with each other. People can believe that child care should be free while also believing that we all pay too much tax. Likewise, people can believe that native title should provide traditional owners with rights over how their lands are utilised, while also believing that Indigenous people's development needs should rank behind the broader community's desire to maintain land in its pristine form.

This presents three big dangers for political leaders who succumb to the blandishments of the pollsters. First, if a politician tries to mirror what the polling says in speeches or interviews, there is a good chance that they will sound confused or incoherent—or worse, deceptive. People might get some reassurance from how the views expressed are familiar, but they will not come away thinking that they have learnt anything.

Second, and more troubling, support for a particular course of action could evaporate. The polling might show that people are willing to pay higher taxes in exchange for better services like education and health, but this might vanish when the question becomes whether or not to trust the government to manage a higher tax take. People are quite capable of keeping two contradictory thoughts in their heads: 'I like government services and I do not trust the government.' Where they come out on this at any point in time is dependent on how the problem is framed and the quality of the advocacy. So the polling can be unhelpful, if not misleading. The real question is what will people think after detailed scrutiny and high levels of emotional advocacy. Only judgement and the anticipation of how competing advocacy will impact opinion is helpful. This is where political leaders earn their keep.

Third, and quite threatening to successful leadership, is the notion that polling is a helpful tool when it comes to making policy decisions designed to address contentious problems. Many problems are hard to resolve without taking actions that hurt some people. Overall, the nation might be a clear winner, but often it is the losers who attract the most attention. In such situations, political leaders can find themselves looking at polling that identifies the measures that the electorate itself thinks would solve the problem. Often, the electorate's solutions are unlikely to work or may even make the problem worse, but they might result in fewer losers. Adopting measures for this reason might seem attractive, because the electorate already appears supportive. At one bound the government appears to have found a solution to its predicament and likely acknowledgement from the electorate that the issue is being addressed. The problem is that governments are held accountable for outcomes. At the end of the day, if a government initiative fails to deliver, it is no defence to say, 'We only did what you suggested!' A strategy based around appearing to deal with a problem is not helpful to the nation and is normally detrimental to ministers.

This is not to say that polling cannot serve a useful purpose. It can be a helpful device for tracking changing community views, which can be empowering for political leaders who see themselves as building community support for change. Having a mechanism to immediately gauge the impact of a new argument can be helpful, as is any indication of how entrenched the views of the community might be.

Regardless, we find ourselves in an odd situation. People are more suspicious of politicians, and the opportunities to engage with them are more fragmented and less effective than they once were. Yet, while it has become more difficult to get people to listen, many political leaders and ministers appear to be going out of their way to be as uninteresting as possible. They will defend whatever it is they are doing, take a swipe at their political opponents, then try and say something that they know from the polling resonates with the electorate. If the polling supports the attack on their political opponents, they will dial it up to a full-throttle roar. And all of this will come from talking points that someone else has written. Most people find listening to a scripted politician an ordeal. People expect a leader to talk about a topic with some candour. When a leader approaches media opportunities in an obviously scripted way, they don't appear to be in charge.

Ministers are often nervous about too much clarification, on the grounds that if they explain too much, they might appear responsible for whatever problem they are talking about, or more worryingly, they might reveal their ignorance of the subject.

Notwithstanding all the research that suggests we have become increasingly unreceptive to reason and prone to view everything as opinion, there is no doubt that a significant proportion of the population is interested in listening to someone who can explain what is going on, and who has a coherent strategy to deal with the problem at hand. The more pressing the problem, the bigger the group willing to listen. This was the basis of Keating's capacity to engage with the nation as treasurer and prime minister. It has been encouraging that, in regard to the response to the COVID-19 pandemic, the approach that worked during the Hawke–Keating years has sprung back to life, to the benefit of the nation and the political leaders involved.

Katharine Murphy's essay 'The End of Certainty' outlines and analyses Australia's response to the pandemic.[30] Reading Murphy's account, it is apparent there are parallels between the coronavirus response and the reforms triggered by the 'banana republic' crisis of May 1986, when Keating as treasurer warned of the demise of the Australian economy. With both, there was a recognised national emergency. With both, there was early political ownership which brought with it an acceptance that there needed to be a response and that the government needed to manage it.

In regard to COVID-19, Prime Minister Morrison, at a March 2020 meeting of the Council of Australian

Governments, took the unprecedented step of creating a National Cabinet comprising the state premiers and territory chief ministers, which, for the early stages of Australia's response, became the main decision-making body in the country. The National Cabinet took a problem-solving approach, not an ideological one. The test was what needed to be done, not what options remained after an ideological filter had been applied. There was an acceptance that, whatever the response, it had to come to grips with the problem. Expert advice on health and economic issues became the order of the day. There was widespread community interest and a great desire to understand what was going on. Notwithstanding the failure of many other countries to respond effectively, and some pushback, there was a willingness in Australia to accept the National Cabinet's role alongside a quite remarkable acceptance of lockdown arrangements. This was a complete break with Australians' recent attitude to government. As Murphy commented, unlike the 2019–20 bushfires, which triggered a wave of anger and activism, the pandemic has led to an upturn in trust in the government, trade unions and business groups, and the perception that governments have been acting competently.[31]

Murphy also commented that the Prime Minister's own approach had evolved, with Morrison becoming more patient, displaying a willingness to persuade and develop a narrative. As a result, there was a steady rebound in his approval ratings over the course of 2020.[32] Morrison was quoted as saying: 'That's what I mean by suspending ideology—you've got to find the right answer.'[33]

Hawke and Keating also approached their task with the belief that they had to find the right answer. The circumstances of the time required transformational change, and while the Hawke–Keating reforms delivered many outcomes that were welcomed by the Labor Party, it is fair to say that the overall approach sat uneasily with many of the party's beliefs. Political parties are complicated coalitions, and it is often the case that the people who have their hands on the levers feel obliged to skew policy towards the ideologies of those whom they feel need placating. But Hawke and Keating were not willing to compromise their end goals. The banana republic imbroglio led to a series of sharp budget cuts as the government refused to put up interest rates in the face of a precipitous fall in commodity prices. In 1987, immediately following the cuts, Hawke called an election, asking for a mandate to see the reform agenda to the end—he won that election quite comfortably.

Hawke's new Cabinet involved a changing of the guard, with a group of ministers with a sentimental attachment to Labor's ideals being replaced by a group of ministers from the Left, who wanted to have something to show for an extended period in government. The understanding was that they needed to support the broad, market-based approach of Keating and Hawke, and in exchange there would be opportunities for reform elsewhere.[34] In this way, the Labor Party coalesced around its successful leadership team. Hawke and Keating articulated their vision for Australia and took pride in delivering Labor's goals while running a market economy more efficiently than their political opponents. The changed attitude of the new ministers in turn ushered in a new phase of reform, giving the government fresh momentum.

The current belief that we have done well during the coronavirus pandemic is reflected in Murphy's inclusion in her essay of a discussion of Australian exceptionalism.[35] Some might see this notion as national hubris writ large and conclude that the bar must be set very low if we are now viewing ourselves in that way. However, Australian exceptionalism is an interesting thought, one worth examining not for reasons of national triumphalism but to identify what might make us so.

Exceptionalism has a confused history in the United States, where political leaders and parties have at times embraced it. For the Americans, it carries the belief that their country follows a path of history different from that on which other countries tread. In recent times, it has provided a convenient divider between those who want to Make America Great Again and those who believe that America has always been exceptional because of its institutions, its traditions and its embedded freedoms. From the perspective of American exceptionalism, any problems now come from the debasement of these three things.

In Australia, we should not simply celebrate our capacity to deal with the COVID-19 pandemic as evidence of our innate, and superior, capability to solve problems. Rather, we need to carefully examine why Australian society responded well to a rational, coherent response delivered by its political leadership. This is important because significant sections of our society face major dislocation in the years ahead, and as we plot a course to economic recovery, we need to be careful that we don't undo the basis of what might make us exceptional.

The early twenty-first century has been a wretched time for many advanced economies, with stagnant real wages and widening inequality opening deep divisions in many societies. It has been suggested that the reality of how many people live is no longer captured by objective indicators of progress such as gross domestic product growth. The lives of many are being shaped by a different set of circumstances, including a health experience which is resulting in a lower life expectancy and in some cases heightened levels of physical and psychological pain.[36] As the groups of those affected expand, it becomes increasingly difficult to maintain a cohesive society, and a country's political leadership starts to fray. This has been the experience of many countries during the pandemic. Australia's ability to frame a rational response and maintain social cohesion is directly linked to the absence of large groups of people who feel alienated and disaffected, and it is testimony to our history of a strong safety net. One of the goals of the recovery should be to ensure that this remains the case. Failure on this front would see any notion that we are exceptional disappear.

Developments with ministerial staff, the public service and communicating with the public have made life more difficult for ministers. Their staff are now more focused on the immediate, the relationship between ministers' offices and the public service is more adversarial, and ministers find it more difficult to be heard. All of this has made it harder for ministers to play a leadership role of the kind that brought great success to the country during the Hawke–Keating years. That said, in considering the communication task that ministers now face, it can be observed that the events surrounding COVID-19 have turned everything upside down and that the approach to dealing with the crisis has parallels with that taken by Hawke and Keating.

The question now is whether the success of the coronavirus response will be the breakthrough that restores Australian political leadership, or whether more is involved. The final piece of the jigsaw is a better understanding of the political strategy of the Hawke–Keating years. But before we turn to that, consideration should be given to examples of how current political attitudes have led to disappointing outcomes.

CLEAN ENERGY

I took up my role as secretary of the Department of Innovation, Industry, Science and Research at the end of June 2011. Apart from the occasional visit to Canberra, I had not had much to do with the city since 1996 and I suffered a strange combination of cultural shock and disorienting familiarity. Ghosts were lurking in every corner of town, particularly around Parliament House. I found myself sitting in the same rooms I had occupied twenty years earlier. A week after I started, I was back in the Australian Embassy in Washington with my new minister Kim Carr, looking at my photo outside the ambassador's office. It was that sort of introduction to my new job. But what really stuck in my mind was the pile of Cabinet submissions on my desk that confronted me in my first week in the office. The submissions covered the government's new plan for a Clean Energy Future and they made quite a stack. The amount of work involved seemed enormous. Every conceivable aspect of the plan, including compensation and unanticipated consequences, appeared to have been pursued or modelled. I did not remember anything on this scale associated with the tax reforms of twenty-five years earlier. It was a clever package which was going to become even more familiar when responsibility for climate change was rolled into my department at the beginning of 2013.

While I was away in Washington, the plan was approved by Cabinet, and when I got back it was due to be announced at a press conference held by prime minister Gillard, treasurer Wayne Swan, and the minister for energy and climate change, Greg Combet. I recall that, in response, the then leader of the Opposition, Tony Abbott, stood under a tree and spoke off-the-cuff, claiming that the government's new plan would have a diabolical impact on the country. The news media gave similar weight to both events. From their perspective, the views expressed at both press conferences were as legitimate as each other. All of this was at odds with my time with Keating, when it was assumed that if a treasurer or prime minister spoke on a matter of national importance, with the full weight of official advice behind them, then they carried an additional level of authority.

In announcing the clean energy plan, the government released a 216-page Treasury document which modelled the impact of a carbon price. The foreword stated that 'this is one of the most comprehensive modelling exercises ever conducted in Australia. The Report provides extensive details on the assumptions and frameworks used, with full details provided on the Treasury website.'[37] The report acknowledged eighty-six people by name. The work behind the modelling was a story in itself, but in terms of creating any impact, it was as if it had never existed. If anything, it was a negative, reinforcing in some people's minds how we were in the hands of mysterious technicians with their black-box computer models.

In the world I had re-entered, there had been a rebalancing away from the authority of ministers and official advice towards whomever managed to get noticed, with all voices treated much as each other. It appeared to be a world where ministers were adrift, hoping for the best. Keating would not have stood behind experts and official modelling without having some understanding of it all himself. He would have sought to control the debate and explain what was going on, knowing full well that if anyone queried his conclusions, there was a body of Treasury analysis to back him up. With work of the quality that lay behind the plan for a Clean Energy Future, he would have mastered the detail, found a suitable venue to announce it—probably the parliament, with all the available bells and whistles—and then proselyted the case every day until polling day. Critics would have been rebutted, and the debate would have been constantly brought back to the cleverness of what was being proposed and why it was right for the country. It would have been an exhausting process, but in the end, good ideas would have driven out bad ideas. With Keating, the watchword would have been: 'Be proud of your work.'

After announcing the plan, the Gillard government not only managed to get the legislation through the House, where it did not have a majority, but also had it passed by the Senate by early November 2011. This was a remarkable achievement. By April 2012 the Clean Energy Regulator had been established, and four months later, Greg Combet and the European Union (EU) commissioner for climate action, Connie Hedegaard, announced that an interim one-way link between Australia's carbon pricing mechanism and the EU Emissions Trading System would commence on 1 July 2015, with a direct link to be established no later than 1 July 2018. Signing the arrangement with the EU meant that the price of carbon in Australia could never diverge materially from that in Europe, regardless of how ambitious any future Australian Parliament might care to be in seeking to reduce emissions. This was a long-run commitment to maintaining the international competitiveness of Australian business, a point not lost on sections of the Business Council of Australia.

At some stage, while talking with one of the advisers from the PMO, I mentioned that people did not seem to fully understand the cleverness of the Clean Energy Future plan, and I thought there was a good story to be told. I was startled when the adviser said that I shouldn't worry. Recent polling had shown that people thought that Abbott would keep the *Clean Energy Act*, that the carbon price was Abbott's issue, and that the government would be talking about education and hospitals, which were its own issues. And in any case, The Greens did not like the idea of buying carbon units offshore. I remember saying that there was only one atmosphere and it did not matter where emissions were reduced around the world. I was shocked. Hearing the same polling-linked story from other senior figures around the parliament only increased my concern.

At the time, all my instincts told me that when the pressure came on, the polling would change and the government would be stranded unless it won the argument over the *Clean Energy Act*. The fact that in October 2011 Abbott made a 'pledge in blood' to repeal the carbon price, and repeated that promise right up to polling day in September 2013, only made me more certain of this.

With the passage of time, I began to understand the new challenges that constrained ministers. I began to accept that moving from a world where the media had been 'one to many' to a world where it was 'many to many' made it difficult to control the debate. I had sympathy for my ministers and the problems with which they now wrestled. However, with Morrison's success in handling the COVID-19 pandemic and the re-establishment of the role of political leaders in a crisis, as well as the new standing this has brought to public officials and agencies, I have become more optimistic that the old verities have not gone forever.

BIG STICK

Another example of a disappointing outcome is the federal government's so-called 'Big Stick' legislation, which was approved by the Senate in November 2019 and came into effect in early June 2020.[38] The intent of the new legislation is to ensure that reductions in wholesale energy costs are passed on to consumers, and that generators and wholesale market participants cannot manipulate electricity prices or cause consumers to pay more than is reasonably necessary. The Australian Competition and Consumer Commission (ACCC), through the Federal Court, will enforce the legislation with a sliding scale of penalties running out to forced divestment. But the magnitude of the penalties and the heightened uncertainty the legislation has created have made it highly contentious with the energy industry.

On the face of it, it might seem odd that the federal government championed this legislation and secured its passage through the parliament. The energy sector is highly capital-intensive, with much of the associated investment long-lived. The risk of stranded assets is high if the relative returns of competing assets change over their lifetimes. The industry has been burdened for many years with the inability of national leaders to agree on a strategy that provides some certainty as to how the emissions intensity of various competing energy sources will be treated when it comes to securing Australia's national emissions reduction targets. For a variety of reasons, it has suited political parties to fight on this issue when the industry requires bipartisan agreement, although even this may now not be enough. The industry needs to anticipate what might happen in the future when the consequences of climate change become even starker and the political response around the world ratchets up. All businesses investing in long-lived energy assets need to work on an assumed shadow price of carbon that will impact their investments at some stage over their lives.

From a South Australian perspective, I am only too familiar with the challenges that the energy company AGL faces in replacing its ageing gas generator assets at Torrens Island. The modelling required to justify new investment is complex, involving assumptions about transmission lines interconnecting with those of other states, the behaviour of grid-scale batteries, the growth of rooftop solar, the growth of grid-scale solar and wind, the future of competing gas-generating assets in South Australia, the life expectancy of coal-fired electricity generation in the eastern states, and the behaviour of the existing three market bodies—the Australian Energy Regulator, the Australian Energy Market Operator, and the Australian Energy Market Commission—that oversight the industry, to say nothing of the behaviour of state and federal energy ministers and what might be happening around the world as the climate changes. With the Big Stick legislation, the industry must now factor in the prospective behaviour of an ACCC newly empowered to ensure that lower wholesale prices are passed on to consumers and to prevent price manipulation in the wholesale market.

The wholesale market is a spot market with a price set every five minutes and averaged every half-hour. It is a complex market where the price moves dramatically over the course of a day. The big three power companies—AGL, Energy Australia, and Origin Energy—have attempted to deal with the volatility and uncertainty of the industry by building vertically integrated businesses and managing a diversified portfolio of generating assets across the country. The integrated energy companies have a natural hedge covering the risk from fixed-price consumer contracts and a volatile spot market. Much of the revenue obtained from generation comes from irregular price spikes driven by an altering balance between supply and demand. The concern for the big three would be that one person's notion of a reasonable return on risk and capital is another person's failure to pass on lower spot prices to consumers; similarly, what might be seen as using a spike in prices as the only means of covering long-run average cost in a market driven by marginal cost pricing, might also be seen as market manipulation. All regulators are keen to see an extension of their powers, but it is not clear that the ACCC has the right understanding of the complexities of the National Electricity Market. It would be understandable if Big Stick has led to energy companies discounting all future revenue flows by an ACCC factor when it comes to considering new investment.

Danny Price is the managing director of Frontier Economics, a consulting business that does considerable work in the areas of climate change and energy. He has been vocal in opposition to Big Stick, saying that it will make Australia so unattractive that it is highly likely that energy companies will lose interest in funding new investment here. Frontier helps companies with market strategies and regulatory reviews, and it has a reputation for rigour and independence—it is often outspoken.

In February 2017, premier Weatherill and then energy minister Tom Koutsantonis announced that they would release a detailed plan on giving South Australia the capacity to proactively influence the stability and security of the state's electricity network. The pressure on Weatherill to respond quickly was strong, but he was keen to give the Cabinet time to properly assess options and craft a coherent plan—Weatherill wanted to find the right answer. Danny Price was contracted to give structure to the analysis and provide Cabinet with independent advice. Price drew attention to the interdependence of the energy system and the importance of not making things worse by taking ill-considered interventionist action.

The final plan was viewed as a considered response to the energy problems facing the state and enabled the Weatherill government to face the 2018 election with answers to a particularly thorny problem.[39]

It is fair to say that when it comes to Big Stick, Danny Price has a point. On top of that, providing the ACCC with the power to force companies to divest sits awkwardly with the philosophical underpinnings of the federal government. Why, then, has the government done something that is likely to make it more difficult for an important sector to invest, while also enshrining a new regulatory power inconsistent with its philosophical beliefs?

Unfortunately, Big Stick has all the hallmarks of a poll-driven policy. Statements made by the Minister for Energy and Emissions Reduction, Angus Taylor, offer a clue. The headline of a September 2019 article by Phillip Coorey and Mark Ludlow in the *AFR*, recording Taylor's response to the Senate passing the legislation, reads: '"Big stick" rules are for the "quiet Australians".' We can read: 'The polling made me do it.' It is true that polling does show that Australians have a jaundiced view of the big energy companies, and that, if asked, they will cheerfully support measures that make the lives of those businesses more difficult. Governments, however, are judged on outcomes, and if companies become less willing to fund the transition to a changing energy environment, that is what people will see and it will be of little consequence that the government did something years earlier with which they agreed.

Ministers often focus on the short term and do not give weight to the longer-term consequences of what they are doing, but in a world where the coronavirus pandemic is accelerating trends, Angus Taylor might find that the gap between now and the future becomes uncomfortably small. This level of discomfort could be aggravated if he has a prime minister with a developing appetite to get policy right.

HAWKE–KEATING 101

Hawke and Keating were in office for thirteen years from 1983 to 1996, winning five elections in a row. Governments are constantly buffeted by events and are frequently knocked off course. However, Hawke and Keating managed to maintain a consistency of approach which is surprising given their long period in office and the complexity of the challenges they faced—the performances of more recent prime ministers looks disorganised in comparison. From the beginning, they instinctively defined what they were doing by linking it to the confronting issue of the moment. They were always seeking to control the agenda. Meeting with John Stone, the then Treasury secretary, the day after the 1983 election, Hawke and Keating were told that Malcolm Fraser and John Howard had officiated over an alarming and unprecedented deterioration in the budget situation; there was also a huge capital outflow that necessitated a substantial devaluation of the Australian dollar. Within four days, they had abandoned Labor's economic program, giving them a clean slate to deal with what was now the key issue facing the nation.[40] Most importantly, it put them in control.

Hawke and Keating were always striving for the approach of 'This is what we are going to talk about', rather than 'What would you like to talk about?' With this objective, they were opposites to the poll-driven political leaders who were keen to talk about matters that might please the electorate. The electorate will only cede to political leadership the right to select the topic of national discourse if that topic involves a recognised countrywide problem—and the price of handing over that right is, of course, the expectation that the problem will be fixed. A poll-driven political leader, keen not to disturb the electorate, would normally be chary about entering into such an arrangement. They would only be willing to embrace a problem if the polling also showed there was a relatively low-cost way of appearing to deal with it.

Identifying a problem and then doing the hard work to fix it had two benefits that made it such an effective political strategy for Hawke and Keating. First, once opinion-formers and the nation more broadly accepted that the identified problem was indeed an important national challenge, the energy around that issue and the strategy developed to deal with it tended to marginalise other issues. This meant that the price of entering the debate was a credible plan to deal with the accepted challenge. For the Opposition, it meant that they had to operate within the framework that Hawke and Keating had established. Given that the strategy had a heavy market emphasis, it was difficult for the Opposition to do other than criticise the government for the slowness of the speed of adjustment, which suited Hawke and Keating well, as at each election it gave them the opportunity to label their political opponents as extremists.[41] Drawing attention away from other issues also made it that much easier to deal with all the messy problems that inevitably surface during the life of any government.

The big bonus of the Hawke–Keating approach was, of course, the right to claim success. It is true that people had higher expectations of government in those days, but recognised success provided a fillip to the Hawke–Keating government, which again stood them in good stead at each election. The current level of disdain directed towards government means that the bar is now so low that governments only need to deliver a modicum of success for the electorate to be astounded. It is to be hoped that the current recognised success that governments have achieved through their management of COVID-19 might lead them to want more. Working through that might surprise political leaders and provide personal satisfaction, good outcomes for the nation and longer political careers.

Over the Hawke–Keating years, the challenges facing the nation changed, but the approach remained essentially the same. At the beginning it was the need to internationalise a moribund Australian economy. Then, during the banana republic period, it was the need to adjust the national call on resources to reflect the collapse in commodity prices. Then, for the 1990 election, it was high interest rates and who was better placed to reduce them while continuing the reform agenda. In 1993, the issue was high unemployment and who had the better plan to address it. It is telling that in the 1996 election, which Keating lost, the challenge was ill-defined, and the Opposition was able to campaign successfully on 'Change the rider, keep the horse'.

Beneath these high-level challenges, there was a raft of other problems identified and dealt with by ministers that added to the overall impression that the Hawke–Keating government was competent and provided a useful service to the nation.[42] All of this required constant and imaginative attention to policy-making. The public service needed to be energised, but it also required creative input from ministers and their advisers—a successful minister needed to understand their portfolio and have a compelling plan.

In a nutshell, Hawke–Keating 101 involved identifying a national challenge, securing the support of opinion-formers on how the challenge was indeed an important one, focusing attention on what needed to be done, assembling a coalition in support, encouraging the recalcitrant to join the coalition and participate in crafting the solution, and then hammering home an outcome. It was important that the solution was fit for purpose. And to be successful, the process had to address real problems; it could not be reform for reform's sake, and the problems embraced had to be acknowledged by ministers, not imposed upon them by others.

Hawke and Keating were quite different personalities, but what made their relationship unusual was the degree of cooperation and mutual support they gave each other for most of their time together. It can frustrate prime ministers, but they cannot expect to usurp the role of their ministers. Governments need a select number of talented ministers to take the initiative and step up. Unfortunately, many prime ministers find such behaviour in their treasurers threatening—we tend to get timorous treasurers or frustrated ones. What distinguished Hawke was that he saw Keating's policy ambition as adding to his own reputation, and so he gave the treasurer his backing. Keating reciprocated, often supporting Hawke on non-economic policies the PM was committed to. Keating's agenda for the country sat very comfortably with Hawke's agenda.

Whether it was intuitive or strategic, both men found it beneficial to support each other—until the one issue that divided them could no longer be ignored. And that, of course, was the leadership. It is unclear whether Hawke ever planned to honour the Kirribilli agreement, but the personality trait that enabled him to see Keating's success as his success also prevented him from seeing how dependent he was on Keating.[43] The result was a leadership spill rather than a dignified handover. This outcome provided Keating with a honeymoon period and the opportunity to fight the 1993 election, in the midst of a recession, on the basis of who had the better plan, rather than who was responsible for the mess. It also allowed him, in the run-up to that election, to give greater structure to his vision for Australia, including Indigenous reconciliation, Australia's role in our region, and our national identity.

Hawke and Keating renewed their relationship before Hawke's death in May 2019, which gave the two men the opportunity to once again share the extraordinary success that they had had together, a success which helped build modern Australia.

SUPERANNUATION: CHANGING LIVES

It has been said that Hawke and Keating took too much official advice. It is true that the Treasury and the Reserve Bank were highly influential during that period, but the main factor was a shared sense that Australia needed to make fundamental economic reforms, and an agreement that those reforms had to be market based. It is interesting, however, to consider superannuation as an example of a policy initiative that did not have great support from the Official Family.[44] Curiously, superannuation continues to generate excited debate even though the legislation for the Superannuation Guarantee (SG) was passed in 1992 and the size of the pool has now reached $3 trillion.

Superannuation grew out of a negotiated process within what was a centralised wage-fixing system. Early on, it became apparent that legislation would be required if the system was to provide universal coverage. On a parallel course, Brian Howe, the minister for social security, was conducting an extensive retirement income review, attempting to address growing concerns about an ageing population and the retirement needs of the baby boomers—it was generally accepted that the boomers would not retire quietly on 25 per cent of average weekly earnings. The two groups tended to view the situation differently. Those who saw superannuation as an industrial issue were conscious of the fact that high-income earners already had superannuation, and they believed that this should be extended to the whole workforce. Those with a social policy perspective tended to be attracted to a government-run national scheme similar to those overseas, where a compulsory levy on workers is invested for them and the workers receive a defined benefit underwritten by the government.

Keating was not attracted to a government-run national superannuation scheme, distrusting the government's capacity to manage the money and reluctant to expose future governments to potentially large unfunded liabilities.[45] But he was attracted to superannuation that ended up in peoples' own accounts, for their use, at their discretion. The only support for a national superannuation scheme came from the Left, which was attracted to the notion of a large government fund capable of giving direction to the federal economy and pension streams at the discretion of the government.

Extending superannuation to the whole workforce and increasing the rate was a key priority of the Australian Council of Trade Unions (ACTU), and Bill Kelty in particular.[46] It was an important topic for discussion between the Accord partners.[47] Keating's interest in superannuation grew as the need for legislation put the Commonwealth's involvement centrestage.[48] The weakness of Australia's financial system had been a core concern of the Hawke–Keating government from the beginning. The folly of the banks during the boom of the late 1980s had been a great disappointment to Keating. Accordingly, the notion that superannuation would deepen Australia's capital market by building a large pool of assets was attractive, as was the notion that national savings would rise as the superannuation rate was progressively lifted. A paucity of national savings bedevilled the nation for all of Keating's time as treasurer, leading to ongoing issues with the current account and the budget deficit. A measure that deliberately encouraged saving and moved the economy away from current consumption towards future consumption was seen as an important structural change inspiring growth.[49]

What excited Keating and Kelty was the notion that compulsory superannuation had the potential to change peoples' lives. Rather than existing on the government pension and living hand to mouth, people with superannuation would have options that came from having financial assets, a privilege held only by the affluent at the time.

However, there was opposition to compulsory superannuation. There were those who saw it as a Treasury-saving device to make working people pay for their own pensions. There were also those who believed that financial services companies would help themselves to unwarranted fees. These people were naturally attracted to a national superannuation scheme along the lines outlined in the Hancock Review of 1976.[50] Brian Howe's decision to support Keating and reject such a scheme was pivotal and meant that opponents of the SG had nowhere else to go.[51]

Having rejected a big government fund, Keating entertained a decentralised competitive model when it came to managing the money and interacting with the members. However, he had no great confidence that private financial services companies, on their own, would deliver sufficient competition to hold down costs. The industry funds were deliberately conceived as a disruptive influence that over time would bring strong competition and innovative investment strategies to the sector. Keating thought from the start that these funds were the future, and he went to some trouble to ensure that they had the right governance structure. There were many lobbying him otherwise, but he insisted that there be equal employer/employee representation on all boards. In this way, he was confident that the one thing the two sides could agree on was that the members came first.

The one group that was largely quiet throughout this period was the Opposition.[52] Much later, Jim Carlton, who was shadow treasurer during Keating's time and an influential member of the Liberal dries, told me that he had argued in support of the SG legislation.[53] He said that there was support in the Liberal Party for the approach by those who appreciated that the SG did not involve a big government fund but rather was fully funded and privately managed. The SG also reduced community dependence on the government. The SG's encouragement of self-provision and self-reliance was an important positive.

Keating had many successes in building broad coalitions to deliver important national objectives. His achievement with superannuation is on a scale that dwarfs what he accomplished elsewhere. The goals are so varied and ambitious and the coalition so diverse that it can only rank as a most extraordinary example of political engineering and ingenuity. It is also a reminder that a precondition for success is a political leader who wants to lead and achieve outcomes.

Which makes current opposition to the SG by certain sections of the Liberal Party puzzling. It is unlikely that current Liberal attitudes are poll-driven, as most polling shows broad public support for superannuation. It is also hard to see the practical benefit of unravelling a mechanism designed to lift long-term national savings and self-provision. The pressures on the government to fund aged care and health are extreme. In an uncertain world, with many people facing insecure employment post sixty, it will be difficult for governments to support those who cannot look after themselves without also having to support those who can provide for themselves. Joining Keating's opponents on the Left and supporting a national superannuation scheme as outlined in the Hancock Review is quite peculiar, as is support for the Future Fund to manage the money.[54] National superannuation is big government writ large, and the Future Fund is a high-cost manager with an investment strategy approved by the minister of finance.[55]

DOING, NOT PLEASING

Many people are nostalgic for the Hawke–Keating years and are dismissive of the quality of recent governments. I have known many ministers, extending from the Hawke–Keating governments to my time in Canberra during the Gillard–Rudd years, and more recently in Adelaide with the Weatherill government.

There were some exceptional characters from the Hawke–Keating period, most notably Hawke and Keating themselves, but I do not subscribe to the notion that somehow ministers are now innately less able to contribute. Many of the ministers I have known more recently are dedicated and talented individuals who would very much like to contribute. The problem is that the framework that surrounds them often constrains their behaviour.

The problem has many dimensions. For a start, there is disagreement about what builds public support and re-election chances. There are those who believe that the path to electoral success becomes clear via problem-solving. These are the doers of my classification. Then there are those who believe that the key to success is translating the wishes of the public into government action. These are the pleasers.

My answer is that the world belongs to the problem-solvers, because in the end the pleasers will be seen as ineffectual and deceptive.

Success requires a change of attitude and a realisation that politics is a battle of ideas around issues that the electorate deems important. Political leaders who can frame an issue in a compelling way and add to public understanding will achieve ascendancy over opponents who cannot. Gaining a reputation as a person with something to say is valuable. Conversely, it is destructive to a politician's reputation to appear to be scripted, with nothing much more to say than to argue that black is white.

Critical to all this is the requirement that a political leader actually wants to lead, that they have the courage to put themselves forward, to become the authority figure, with the power to make decisions and draw responsibility to them.

With a change of attitude and political leadership that wants to step up, there is the hope of success. However, ministers, premiers and prime ministers are only as good as the advice infrastructure and disciplines around them. Ministerial staff were an important development during the Hawke–Keating years, but they are no longer fit for purpose. Moreover, the relationships between ministers, their offices and the public service are often needlessly adversarial. More can be done by including trusted, experienced public servants in a minister's office, and if secretaries strengthen their departments and build more effective and trusting relationships with their ministers. If change of this nature is to happen, it will stem from the realisation by prime ministers and premiers that this is the best way to deliver successful outcomes for themselves and their governments.

All of this said, it has become more difficult for ministers to communicate. This does not negate the point that the public will still listen if they deem the topic worthy of their attention. It just means that ministers need to be highly alert to topics of public interest.

At present, the national recovery from the COVID-19 recession is of considerable public interest. This topic warrants the same successful problem-solving approach evident in the early stages of the nation's response to the pandemic itself. Rebuilding and expanding existing industries and encouraging the development of new ones is in many ways more challenging and complex than the big reforms of the 1980s and 1990s, which were all about making the Australian economy internationally competitive.[56] The new economic challenge requires drawing on the range of skills and resources that exist in the public sector and which can strengthen and invigorate private business. These skills and resources can also reinforce growth areas such as health, disabilities and aged care that are underpinned by the public sector. Universities, science, research and skills development, and how these translate effectively across the economy, will be the key to how we fare.

The Australian people will reward whomever can make sense of all this and rise to the occasion.

TABLE 1: COMMONWEALTH AND SOUTH AUSTRALIAN MINISTERS, 2011–18

CANBERRA		
Kim Carr	Innovation, Industry, Science and Research	13 Dec 2007 – 13 Dec 2011
	Manufacturing	14 Dec 2011 – 4 Mar 2012
	Innovation, Industry, Science and Research	1 July 2013 – 18 Sep 2013
	Higher Education	1 July 2013 – 18 Sep 2013
Nick Sherry	Small Business	14 Sept 2010 – 14 Dec 2011
Mark Arbib	Small Business	14 Dec 2011 – 5 Mar 2012
Greg Combet	Industry and Innovation	14 Dec 2011 – 25 Mar 2013
	Climate Change, Industry and Innovation	25 Mar 2013 – 1 July 2013
Chris Evans	Tertiary Education, Skills, Science and Research	14 Dec 2011 – 4 Feb 2013
Chris Bowen	Tertiary Education, Skills, Science and Research	4 Feb 2013 – 25 Mar 2013
	Small Business	4 Feb 2013 – 25 Mar 2013
Brendan O'Connor	Small Business	5 Mar 2012 – 4 Feb 2013
	Skills and Training	1 July 2013 – 18 Sep 2013

Craig Emerson	Tertiary Education, Skills, Science and Research	25 Mar 2013 – 1 July 2013
Don Farrell	Science and Research	25 Mar 2013 – 1 July 2013
Sharon Bird	Higher Education and Skills	25 Mar 2013 – 1 July 2013
Gary Gray	Small Business	25 Mar 2013 – 18 Sep 2013
Mark Butler	Climate Change	1 July 2013 – 18 Sep 2013
ADELAIDE		
Gail Gago	Employment, Higher Education and Skills	26 Mar 2014 – 18 Jan 2016
	Science and Information Economy	26 Mar 2014 – 18 Jan 2016
Tom Koutsantonis	State Development	26 Mar 2014 – 19 Mar 2018
	Mineral Resources and Energy	26 Mar 2014 – 19 Mar 2018
	Small Business	26 Mar 2014 – 18 Jan 2016
	Automotive Transformation	26 Mar 2014 – 27 May 2014
Susan Close	Manufacturing, Innovation and Trade	26 Mar 2014 – 27 May 2014
	Manufacturing and Innovation	27 May 2014 – 3 Feb 2015
	Automotive Transformation	27 May 2014 – 3 Feb 2015
	Higher Education and Skills	19 Jan 2016 19 Mar 2018

Martin Hamilton-Smith	Investment and Trade	27 May 2014 – 18 Jan 2018
	Small Business	19 Jan 2016 – 18 Jan 2018
	Health Industries	18 Sep 2017 – 18 Jan 2018
Jack Snelling	Arts	26 Mar 2014 – 17 Sep 2017
	Health Industries	26 Mar 2014 – 17 Sep 2017
Ian Hunter	Aboriginal Affairs and Reconciliation	21 Jan 2013 – 3 Feb 2015
Kyam Maher	Employment	19 Jan 2016 – 19 Mar 2018
	Aboriginal Affairs and Reconciliation	3 Feb 2015 – 19 Mar 2018
	Manufacturing and Innovation	3 Feb 2015 – 19 Mar 2018
	Automotive Transformation	3 Feb 2015 – 19 Mar 2018
	Science and Information Economy	19 Jan 2016 – 19 Mar 2018
Jay Weatherill	Premier	21 Oct 2011 – 19 Mar 2018
	Arts	18 Sep 2017 – 19 Mar 2018
John Rau	Public Sector	19 Jan 2016 – 19 Mar 2018

TABLE 2: COMMONWEALTH SECRETARIES, AS AT OCTOBER 2020

Department of Agriculture, Water and the Environment	Andrew Metcalfe AO
Attorney-General's Department	Chris Moraitis PSM
Department of Defence	Greg Moriarty
Department of Education, Skills and Employment	Michelle Bruniges AM
Department of Finance	Rosemary Huxtable PSM
Department of Foreign Affairs and Trade	Frances Adamson
Department of Health	Brendan Murphy
Department of Home Affairs	Michael Pezzullo
Department of Industry, Science, Energy and Resources	David Fredericks
Department of Infrastructure, Transport, Regional Development and Communications	Simon Atkinson
Department of the Prime Minister and Cabinet	Philip Gaetjens
Department of Social Services	Kathryn Campbell AO CSC
Department of the Treasury	Steven Kennedy PSM
Department of Veterans' Affairs	Liz Cosson AM CSC

ACKNOWLEDGEMENTS

I want to thank Paul Keating, Julia Gillard and Jay Weatherill for having trust in me. Without them, there would be no book.

My thanks also to Louise Adler, the series editor, who saw the need for this book and provided insightful and thoughtful guidance. Thanks to Paul Smitz, the series coordinator and copyeditor, for his clarity and inspired capacity to discard words while enhancing meaning.

And last but not least, I thank my wife Lisa Barker, for the tireless enthusiasm with which she greets each new task I take on, and the endless support she has always given me.

NOTES

1 Table 1 at the back of this book lists the ministers, their titles and appointment dates.

2 The two independents were Geoff Brock, a former mayor of Port Pirie, and Martin Hamilton-Smith, a former leader of the Liberal Party.

3 Dr Don Russell, 'Reflections on My Time in Canberra', Crawford School Reflections Lecture, ANU, Canberra, 31 March 2014.

4 Department of Finance estimates.

5 Department of the Prime Minister and Cabinet, *Our Public Service Our Future: Independent Review of the Australian Public Service*, Australian Government, Canberra, 13 December 2019, p. 134.

6 An Australia and New Zealand School of Government (ANZSOG) research paper for the APS Review Panel comments on the declining number of public servants moving to and from ministerial offices as matter of concern; see Anne Tiernan, Ian Holland and Jacob Deem, 'Being a Trusted and Respected Partner: The APS' Relationship with Ministers and their Offices', ANZSOG research paper, March 2019.

7 Conversations with the author.

8 In 1993, Keating had five people with doctorates working in the PMO.

9 See Maria Maley, 'Temporary Partisans, Tagged Officers or Impartial Professionals: Moving between Ministerial Offices and Departments', *Public Administration*, vol. 95, no. 1, 2017, pp. 407–20.

10 Ibid.

11 Department of the Prime Minister and Cabinet, *Delivering for Australians: A World-Class Australian Public Service—The Government's APS Reform Agenda*, Australian Government, Canberra, 13 December 2019.

12 Department of the Prime Minister and Cabinet, *Our Public Service Our Future*.

13 When I was travelling with some Western Australian colleagues in the Pilbara in 2013, they cheerfully told me of a time when state ministers would need to make an appointment to meet with a director-general. Now the directors-general wait in line to meet with a minister.

14 The PM provided an additional $15.1 million. The APSC has a responsibility to lift the quality and professionalism of the APS, but it has struggled in recent years with limited funding. The Secretaries Board is chaired by the secretary of PM&C; its role is already enshrined in the *Public Service Act*.

15 I worked with SA premier Weatherill on a framework which would set out the responsibilities of the minister and the departmental chief executive (CE) and their relative accountabilities. It required the minister to be satisfied that the CE had in place a risk-management framework to deal with current and developing problems, and for the CE and the minister to maintain an informed and trusted relationship, a set of arrangements that had to involve the head of the premier's department.

16 Russell, 'Reflections on My Time in Canberra'.

17 The Senior Management Council is the SA version of the Commonwealth Secretaries Board, differing in that it includes the police commissioner—given the importance of policing to departments, this is a sensible addition. The head of the premier's department chairs the State Emergency Management Committee, which includes the SA Police, Metropolitan Fire Service, Country Fire Service, State Emergency Service, and the Fire and Emergency Services Commission. The police commissioner has overall operational control in an emergency; there is also an Emergency Management Council chaired by the premier.

18 Andrew Metcalfe is now the Secretary of the Department of Agriculture, Water and the Environment. In September 2013, he was terminated as the secretary of the Department of Agriculture, Fisheries and Forestry by the incoming Tony Abbott government.

19 It is true that ministers prefer a separate department with their own secretary, but that is not how prime ministers and premiers want to run their governments. This means that a secretary

needs to be able to work effectively with several ministers at the same time.

20 This second capability is more complicated than it might sound. Traditionally, a secretary has had only one line of responsibility, which is to their minister. However, ministers and prime ministers do not always agree, and there are times when the prime minister needs to be aware of what is going on. For a secretary to talk to the head of PM&C about their minister requires careful judgement.

21 See Table 2 at the end of this book, which lists the current Commonwealth secretaries.

22 Daniel Kahneman, *Thinking, Fast and Slow*, Penguin Books, London, 2012.

23 Gareth Evans, *Inside the Hawke–Keating Government: A Cabinet Diary*, Melbourne University Press, Melbourne, 2014.

24 Ibid., 'Introduction'.

25 The fact that Hawke continued to appoint senior public servants to head up the PMO after the departure of Graham Evans reinforces this belief.

26 People such as Don Watson, Bruce Chapman and Anne Summers drove imaginative policy innovation during their time.

27 I remember Dr Ian Watt, as secretary of PM&C and chair of the Secretaries Board, telling us that all secretaries should have a plan B in their pocket, and no-one should see themselves as a secretary for life. I have always thought that there is scope for people to move in and out of the secretary role, building up experience elsewhere to recharge their batteries and further strengthen their capabilities.

28 Kahneman, *Thinking, Fast and Slow*, p. 53.

29 Ibid., p. 209.

30 Katharine Murphy, 'The End of Certainty: Scott Morrison & Pandemic Politics', *Quarterly Essay*, no. 79, 2020.

31 Ibid., pp. 89, 90.

32 Ibid., p. 65.

33 Ibid., p. 73.

34 Arthur Gietzelt and Tom Uren left the ministry, and Gerry Hand and Nick Bolkus joined it. Keating developed a productive relationship with Brian Howe, who obtained Cabinet approval for proposals that included the Child Support Agency and the Family

Allowance Supplement, with Keating's support. Howe was also supportive of the Superannuation Guarantee.

35 Murphy, 'The End of Certainty', p. 80. Murphy puts forward the notion that there are potential prizes for anyone who can incorporate Australian exceptionalism into their political narrative for the country.

36 William Davies, *Nervous States: How Feeling Took over the World*, Vintage Books, London, 2018.

37 The Treasury, *Strong Growth Low Pollution: Modelling a Carbon Price*, Australian Government, Canberra, 10 July 2011.

38 *The Treasury Laws Amendment (Prohibiting Energy Market Misconduct) Act 2019*.

39 The Energy Plan was released on 14 March 2017.

40 Paul Kelly, *The End of Certainty*, rev. edn, Allen & Unwin, St Leonards, NSW, 1994.

41 It was difficult for the Opposition to walk away from the market-based strategy of the government, as John Howard and the economic rationalists were criticising Andrew Peacock, Howard's leadership rival, as a 'wet'.

42 The recognised accomplishments included Brian Howe with the Child Support Agency and the Family Allowance Supplement; John Dawkins with the Higher Education Contribution Scheme; Gareth Evans with the Cambodian peace process; John Button with tariff reform; John Kerin with the deregulation of agriculture; Neal Blewett with Medicare and the HIV/AIDS campaign; Kim Beazley with defence and the submarine program; Lionel Bowen with reform of corporations law; Susan Ryan with the *Sex Discrimination Act*; Nick Bolkus with privacy legislation; Graham Richardson with the protection of national heritage; and Paul Keating with tax reform, decentralising the labour market, the Asia-Pacific Economic Cooperation leaders' meeting, and superannuation. (I will cover superannuation in the next section.)

43 In late 1988, Hawke agreed with Keating at the PM's residence at Kirribilli that he would hand over the leadership after the next election. The arrangement was witnessed by Sir Peter Abeles and Bill Kelty.

44 Keating referred to the Treasury and the Reserve Bank as the 'Official Family'.

45 The collapse of the State Bank of Victoria in 1990 and the State Bank of South Australia in 1991 reinforced doubts about the capacity of governments to manage an investment portfolio.
46 Bill Kelty was secretary of the ACTU from 1983 to 2000.
47 The Prices and Incomes Accord was an agreement between the ACTU and the Hawke–Keating government to restrict wage demands in exchange for action on the social wage and tax cuts. Much of its energy and effectiveness came from the close working relationship between Keating and Kelty.
48 The decision of the Industrial Relations Commission to defer another 3 per cent superannuation round added pressure on the Commonwealth to legislate.
49 Vince W FitzGerald, *National Saving: A Report to the Treasurer*, Australian Government Publishing Service, June 1993. FitzGerald was a consultant to the Keating government in 1992.
50 National Superannuation Committee of Inquiry, *Final Report of the National Superannuation Committee of Inquiry*, Australian Government Publishing Service, Canberra, 1976. The majority recommendation provided for a contributory scheme that would sit on top of the government pension; it would be a defined benefit underwritten by the government. The minority recommendation dismissed a national superannuation scheme, concerned that it would undermine the existing needs-based government pension.
51 Brian Howe, 'Better Incomes: Retirement Income Policy into the Next Century', Australian Government Publishing Service, Canberra, 1989. Howe was the principal minister of the Left in the Hawke ministry at the time.
52 Opposition acceptance of the SG was important to Keating because the timeline for implementation ran out to 2002. A change of government could threaten this.
53 Conversations with the author.
54 Andrew Bragg, *Bad Egg: How to Fix Super*, Connor Court, Brisbane, 2020.
55 The potential distorting influence of government on the investment decisions of the Future Fund has always been a concern. The Future Fund solution is to outsource the process to professional managers, many of whom are high-cost.
56 Russell, 'Reflections on My Time in Canberra'.

IN THE NATIONAL INTEREST

Other books on the issues that matter:

Bill Bowtell *Unmasked: The Politics of Pandemics*

Rachel Doyle *Power & Consent*

Martin Parkinson *A Decade of Drift*

Kevin Rudd *The Case for Courage*

Scott Ryan *Challenging Politics*

Simon Wilkie *The Digital Revolution: A Survival Guide*